Beneath the Surface

By Ben Douglass

FIRST EDITION
Mercury Flats Publishing
Portland, Oregon. USA

Mercury Flats Publishing is a Portland, Oregon based sole
proprietor business (DBA #1056590-98) that manages the
intellectual properties of Ronald Dwayne Douglass, also known as
Benjamin Douglass, Ben Douglass and Dizzy Douglass.

ISBN: 978-0-578-79355-9

Front cover photo credit: Willow Springs, California. 2012.

Printed in the United States of America by Amazon KDP.

Dedication

Willy Marks
1919-2005
Chemehuevi Native Elder
Alamosa, Colorado

"You'll never find life in the shining light of day.
Real life will always lurk just <u>beneath the surface</u>.
Always look for it there, no matter what anyone
else tells you."

Enlightenment is the emancipation of man from a state of self-imposed tutelage. This state is due to his incapacity to use his own intelligence without external guidance. Such a state of tutelage I call self-imposed (or culpable) if it is due not to lack of intelligence but to lack of courage or determination to use one's own intelligence without the help of a leader. Saper aude! Dare to use your own intelligence! That is the battle cry of the Enlightenment.

Immanual Kant
Essay: What is Enlightenment

CONTENTS

Author's Preface

The narrative poem, "The Boy from Twentynine Palms," was first conceived and written in the summer of 1982, after a year-long study of the area and its native peoples. The poem was then re-written in prose as the "Twenty Dollar Boy," and became a story within a story in my 2017 novella, *This Ain't the Waldorf Astoria, Honey!* In 2019 I revisited the original poem and added the last stanza. "Desert Meditations" is the result of my many travels alone in the Mojave Desert from 1980-82, while living in Tehachapi, California. "Walkabout" is a collection of poems that were specifically inspired by my further studies of the Chemehuevi Peoples, and further adventures in the Mojave Desert area near California City, Boron, Pear Blossom, and the Lucerne Valley in 2007, 2010, 2012, and 2015.

"Our Lady of the Rock" is the result of my visit to Sister Maria Paula Acuna's compound in the Mojave Desert, circa 2016.

Acknowledgements

My biggest and most generous acknowledgement must go to the late Mr. Edgar C. Hoeft, of Tehachapi, California. I worked for him for two years as a mechanics helper at E. & M. Garments. He was the first to introduce me to the wonders of the Mojave Desert through his stories. He even took me on a "drive about," as he called it, in his International jeep to some interesting places outside Tehachapi. And he always encouraged my desire to write and explore the "inner sanctum of the Mojave National Preserve." Next. I must acknowledge the half dozen Chemehuevi men who I had the pleasure of interviewing to learn about their culture. Their stories of Chemehuevi life in the early Twentieth Century inspire me to this day. I owe those men much gratitude.

Introduction

This volume of narrative poems speaks of my deep and abiding spiritual connection with the Mojave Desert in general, and the Chemehuevi Native Peoples specifically. Most of the poems in this collection were composed during periods of great personal crisis and life changing transitions: From fundamentalist Christian, to new ager, to Buddhist, to humanist, and then finally to radical agnostic. The Mojave Desert became, and still is, my Benefactor, Healer and Higher Power.

Like Walt Whitman, my poetry is at once a proclamation of spirituality, individualism and freedom. I compose my poetry, not as a way of earning a living, but that of personal spiritual practice. Poetry as spiritual practice comes in two parts. The first is reading the poems of our civilization, plumbing the depths of abstraction to discover great truths about the world we live in. Secondly, is writing your own poems, making them part and parcel of your daily rituals, aspirations and intentions.

And then by assuming certain attitudes and postures, contemplating and reciting poems, chants, hymns, prayers, mantras, songs, and scripture, you make yourself an open and willing receptacle for life itself.

The one most important lesson I took away from my wanderings in the Mojave Desert (and its human inhabitants) was — *life is a balancing act between interior wishes and ideals, and harsh outer reality.* In 2012, I finally rejected the rigid ideologies of the theist as well as the atheist. Both worldviews are based in a predetermined mythology: one being a panorama of gods and an afterlife, the other being an intractable scientific materialism. I did not want to be associated with either side. My compromise, if you will, was settling on a form of radical agnosticism. This view gave me the freedom to investigate the mysterious unknowns out there without submitting to blind faith or rigid ideology.

My greatest hope is that those who read this volume of narrative poems will understand who I am, appreciate the Great Mojave and its people, and maybe share in the same experience I had, even if vicariously so.

The Boy from Twentynine Palms

Prologue

The early morning sun was strong, warm and inviting. Off in the distance fluffy white clouds paraded across the intensely blue horizon, pushed by the Santa Ana winds, like so many misshapen animals and hulking mountain peaks. It was the kind of morning that invited picnics, games and squealing children. It was one of those mornings that could be talked about over a late evening meal of roasted boar or deer, and a table filled with the laughter of family and friends. And so it was just this kind of morning, on the lush Oasis of Twentynine Palms, located within the circle of the Hidalgo, Aqua, Queen, and San Gorgonia mountains of southern California.

1.

Tomas was happy.
Today was his 12th birthday.
Wildflowers spread their beauty across the land.
It was Spring in the year of our Lord
Nineteen hundred and six.
Father woke him early for his first hunt of wild boar.
Arriving at their destination after hours of walking,
They were met by three white men,
One of them being very tall.
The tall one looked at the boy up and down,
Scratching his chin, and said in a low,
Almost inaudible voice:
"He will do nicely. He has potential."
The tall one thrust a leather pouch into father's hand.
Father greedily counted the thirty silver coins. Father
Gave his son one final look,
While stuffing the pouch under his red shirt,
And walked away.
Tomas was greatly confused. He wanted to run after
Father but, the tall one grabbed him quickly with an
Iron grip that made him wince.
Tomas struggled with all his might but the
Iron grip was impossible to break.
He screamed, begging father to come back.
Father never looked back!

2.

Tomas suffered greatly under the supervision of
These three white men.
He soon learned that he had been sold into
Indentured servitude
To pay off father's gambling and drinking debts.
Tomas grew strong in body due to the hard work,
While his hatred for father grew even stronger.
This hatred kept him going year after year,
Even when he wanted to give up and
Take his own life.

3.

One cold Spring day, on his 16th birthday,
The tall one released Tomas from servitude.
He was finally free!
Tomas' first thought and mission in life was

To find father and kill him. For the next three
Years, Tomas looked high and low. He even
Visited his old homestead.
(Nobody he remembered was there, not even
His folks and two little sisters).
He then got a job on the railroad to earn his keep,
And gained a reputation as a strong, honest worker
Who could be depended upon.

4.

The August day was fiercely hot in
Needles, California.
Tomas decided to stop by the general store for a
Cold sarsaparilla. On the front steps a beggar
Who looked many years beyond his age,
Stood with tin cup.
The man had the appearance of a heavy drinker.
Tomas had seen it before,
And it always disgusted him
How anyone could let themselves be
Taken hostage by liquor. The man was blind, feeble
And supported his thin frame with a pair of crutches.
The old man sensed his presence and asked for a
Pair of quarters. Tomas asked the beggar how he let
Himself get into his present condition. The man
Quickly told his story in hopes of getting money.

5.

"Years ago, I drank heavily and ran up big
Gambling debts with three white men.
When it was time to pony up, I did not have
The money. I ended up selling my only son into

Indentured servitude.
Soon afterward my wife took my two daughters
And deserted me.
I became sorry for what I did and tried to
Find my son but failed.
I drank myself into deep sleep every night
After that. I went blind two years ago from
Bad Whisky. All I can see now are shadows
And forms that are unrecognizable."

6.

Tomas thoughtfully listened to the beggar's story,
And knew that he finally found father.
The murderous rage bottled up all those years
Left him instantly,
After seeing what became of father.
Father asked him again for two quarters.
Tomas looked to the sky momentarily and then
Gave him two silver dollars – half his
Week's wages –
Father grabbed the silver, stumbled into the
Store while Tomas followed.

Tomas bought his cold sarsaparilla and
Thanked the owner. As he lingered at the door,
He saw father buying whisky, hardtack and beans.
Quickly departing the store, without saying
Anything more to father, Tomas walked down the
Street without looking back.
A deep sigh of relief washed over him,
He knew he could now live life unhindered
From his past. Tomas also knew that he would
Never become like father.
He would become his own man,
In his own way, without the help of the
Dice and whisky.

Epilogue

*The late afternoon sun was surrendering to the subtle pinks,
burnt orange and soft red colors of dusk. Off in the distance fluffy
white clouds of all shapes and sizes now took on a grayish, black
hue and seemed to hang there frozen in time like a painting on a
vase. It was the kind of evening that would invite silence, reflection
and staring at warm hearth fires. It was one of those evenings that
would make hearts yearn for the light of a new day. And so it
was just this kind of evening, on the lush Oasis of Twentynine
Palms, located within the circle of the Hidalgo, Aqua, Queen,
and San Gorgonio mountains of southern California.*

High Desert Meditations

Satori

A rosy-fingered dawn breaking
Across the Mojave National Preserve,
Sitting amongst a Congregation of
Beavertail, Silver Cholla, Prickly Pear
And Engelmann hedgehog cactus'.
A chuckwalla rears its head at my foot,
And blinks.
Satori, split-second keep going.

The Mighty Chuckwalla

A little ugly rodent is the
Chuckwalla, but mighty in
Deed,
Pushing before it an old
Dung ball, persistently.
Life in the Great Mojave,
Simple, refined, brilliantly
Showing off its own
Complexity.

Fata Morgana

Route 66
Screaming past inconsequential
Ghost towns
Doing 115 MPH
Up ahead a signpost
Then Fata Morgana appears
Now doing 45 MPH
Pulling full stop on gravel shoulder
Getting out
Staring

Shaking
Prickly skin
Hair standing on end
Temples
Spires
Pagoda's stand
Incredible majesty
Beyond belief
Checking my pulse
Rapid short breaths
BRIGADOON?

Desert Awareness

They say in the desert one can find
Everything and nothing.
Stay aware. Know where you are –
Your biological address.
Know your neighbors –
Plants, creatures, who live there,
Who died there, who is blessed,
Cursed, what is absent or in danger
Or in need of your help.
Pay attention to the weather,
To what breaks your heart,
To what lifts your heart.
Remember.
Write it down.

Seeking Form

Contemplating Gaia's True Form
Just before sunrise, walking
Wide-open, empty spaces,
Ground squirrel runs amok.
The Great Mojave Desert
My deepest passion, pleasure
Of youth.

Leaving

Intensity of burning, searing heat on self,
Brain explodes into melted synapses like
Kraft cheese, as I stumble towards my
Air-conditioned car.
I take one final glance at the
Nothingness over my shoulder:
Clearly, I am missing something!

Cloudburst

Late afternoon cloudburst –
Furnace heat lobbers cling desperately
To trembling creosote bushes.

No Enlightenment

How absurdly noble & wise
Of one who finds no enlightenment
In the flash of lightning
A harsh rain, flash flood
On a Spring day

Breakfast

Breakfast of berries, desert melon,
Prickly pear, succulent leaves
In the fine company of
Desert wildflowers
And sunrise.

Insight

A solitary
Turkey vulture on a bare, strong branch –
October twilight in the Mojave Preserve.

Exhaustion

Exhausted from hours journey to Panamint City,
I yearned for an English Inn, but found
Desert flowers in full bloom.

Middle Age

Like a dark October in the Mojave
Middle age prematurely settles over me
Like heavy rain clouds or
Something unknown to me.

Joy of Life

Long sweet conversations
While sitting among blooming desert
Wildflowers –
Joy of life on the road.

Focused

A beautiful spring morning
Suddenly vanished while I
Viewed desert wildflowers.

Dark Night of Soul

Sick at the end of my journey,
Only my dreams will wander
These desolate spaces of
The Great Mojave National Preserve.

Walkabout

The Roach Motel

Outwardly it is nothing special,
No, by any stretch of the
Imagination, no.
The Roach Motel is a hiding place,
A safe, secure hiding place of
A gathering of lost, broken souls.
Some stay on with memories
Intact, of pain, pleasure, indifference.
Some move on to other places;
Better or same.
Some die without ever knowing WHY.
A few finally see with eyes wide open.
It really is nothing special,
Just home!

Mojave Man

He does not attempt to interpret life,
To explain away death. He accepts
The life and death pattern of existence,
Unquestionably.
And through this acceptance,
Attains enviable strength, peace of mind
And spirit. He is like the
Primitive Man! (of the 19th century)

What You Need to Know

What you need is already in you:

A living, breathing firmament of
Cosmic Wonder;
A sea of suns, planets & moons;
Continents of geologic strata and flower.
The enlightenment you seek, bubbles from
Within the wellsprings of your beating heart.
You need not go anywhere or ask anyone,
Nor read a book or bible.
Stand still, hold fast, hope and listen.
Then you become the world.

The Moment

Singing the salt songs of my
Adopted brothers & sisters – the Chemehuevi,
I tread the ancient path of Earth, Wind & Fire,
(Through the Mojave National Preserve)
Forever seeking the MOMENT right Here and Now,
Forgetting past & future.

The Singing Sands

The singing sands of the Great Mojave boom,
Boom like a thousand voice choir of
Angels, flowing from Heaven's Gate.
The breath of Great Spirit tumbles across
The dunes,
Into the night sky to join their comrades,
Who have gone on before. They will
Return in minutes, hours, days,
Renewed and cleansed of earth-earthy dross,
To begin again.

Monument Rock

Monument Rock, a Cathedral in time,
Stands unfazed before me,
Through epochs, history and generations
Of slime and dust.

I see epitaphs of those who went before me.
I hear the whispers of flower, lizard, bird, wolf.
I taste magna, pumice and lime,
Of the Mother that never sleeps.
I smell the earth and its pungent spice.
I touch the surface of slate and mineral essence.

Bow down before the rock of the ages.
Chant the salt songs of my adopted
Brothers and sisters –
The Chemehuevi.

Dancing on the Waves of Time-space

Sitting on the desert floor, disturbing it not,
Listening to the sermons of the
Pinion jay, screech owl, bat and moth.

The fiery firmament above spins like a great
Wheel of Life in the immense inky darkness,
Churning, churning onward, slowly towards a
Destination not yet known.

With my eyes fixed upon a trembling star,
I am catapulted into the Cosmic Sea, adrift,
Searching for a door to another place, another time,
To meet my other self, to embrace, to acknowledge.

Sitting on the desert floor, deserting it not,
Absorbing the wisdom of sky and earth,
And pinion jay, screech owl, bat and moth.

Be on Your Way

Be on your way old friend.
Across the great starry expanse,
Into the next phase of your
Journey that is just begun.

Be on your way old friend.
The ones left behind will always
Remember the good that you did,
And never once judged another.

Be on your way old friend.
Whatever you become – leaf, rock or star,
In the next incantation of life.
The universe is wiser now that you had lived.

Great Spirit

Not beast, not man, not mind trick.
Nor Earth, Fire or Water. Even the
Moons, planets, stars, solar systems,
And the magnificent galactic firmament
Must take a back seat to Great Spirit.
If you must know, know this –
It starts with hope, becomes redemption and
Finally Self-Realization.
Don't seek it, just be. It always comes
Like a thief in the darkest of nights.
Don't talk about it, don't think about it,
Just listen. The voice will come.
Go about your business, your life, as if in
Constant contemplation. Learn to wait!

The Mighty Joshua Tree

Before me stands an awesome monument
Of Joshua trees. Gangly arms sticking out
Every which way, the oldest and tallest
Propped on woody trunks that look like legs
On the elephant man. Each needle-sharp leaf
Tipped in brown, as if dipped in an inkwell,
And edged with tiny-serrated teeth. Spent
Thatch hangs like a shaggy gray beard
Below the green tops. No wonder that
Early Mormons gave these plants the
Biblical name – to them Joshua trees
Looked like the old prophet pointing the way
As they traveled across the parched Mojave
Or perhaps raising arms to heaven in
Wonder of what they might be doing here
In the first place.

Desert Meditation

As I do my morning walking meditation,
The communities of the Great Mojave Preserve,
Shrub, insect, lizard, rodent, animal, bird
Surround me, welcome me as brother.
Shadscale, desert holly, wolfberry, brittlebush,
Creosote, bursage and Mormon Tea,
Stand against the harsh environment
As shelter, food and protection of all.
Bees, creosote grasshopper, desert clicker
And furnace heat lobber, spread pollen,
Like an army of farmers whose job is to
Feed the teeming, complex community.

Leopard lizards, desert iguana's, chuckwalla's,
Mice, packrats, pocket gophers, kangaroo rats,
Ground squirrels, and bats with their special skills,
Glean the community for balance and permanency.
The desert kit fox. Turkey vulture, tortoise
And raven; the aristocracy of the Mojave,
Watches over the world, night and day,
Giving warning to their followers of human intrusion.

The Borrego Sandman

The Borrego Sandman* stalks me
Night and day relentlessly.
Even my dreams are not
Safe from this beast, no matter
How hard and fast I run,
Or find a clever hiding place.
It shows up always
Casting its long terrible shadow.
It beckons me with open arms,
Only wanting a simple, fast embrace.
The Chemehuevi People say it is a
Bad omen to see the Borrego Sandman,
And even worse if it stalks your dreams.
When this happens death
Is certainly near, so they say.

*The Borrego Sandman is the legendary bigfoot of the Mojave Desert, and roams the sand dunes night and day. It supposedly was first sighted back in 1939 by two gold prospectors, and again in 1959 by an Air Force officer at Edwards Air Base.

Precipice

I stand on a precipice
Not wanting to look down.
The wind at my back
Gently pushing me closer to the edge.
Frozen with fear and dread
A scream ignites deep inside.
I grab my throat with both hands
To stop the inevitable.
Silence maintains its guard.
I cannot breath.
Then darkness...unforgiving darkness.

Meditation at Sand Canyon: May 1998

My father, the long shadow that loomed
Across all the years of my life...died. It took me
Forty years to get out from beneath that shadow
And live my life on my own terms.
One generation passes, another comes,
Gaia endures – if not forever, longer than
The superficial, transient lifestyles and
Systems of sentiments evolved by successive
Races of peoples who dwell upon it.
The Great Mojave Preserve passes slowly, slowly,
Tik Tok...Tik Tok...Tik Tok... [time stands still]
The Great Desert's skin slashed by freeways, torn
By monstrous earth machines and ATVs bearing
Down upon its fragile skin. Manmade oases, strangely
Incongruous resort complexes, it remains vast, empty.
Clouds cast mysterious purple, pink, gray shadows,
Thunderstorms menace, violent rainstorms drench,
Sudden but brief. These also pass, and the desert lies
Pale, still, empty beneath the hot empty
Merciless Sky!

Self Determination

WALKABOUT –
I miss my meandering days
In the Great Mojave Preserve,
During my lonely tour of duty,
Talking to cacti, beetle & snake.
A Great Spiritual Awakening!
DEATH –
Now trapped in the iron grip
Of civilization, people, things
And events [beyond my control],
My soul years for release!
HOME –

When I can no longer resist the urge,
And decide to travel
Beyond the Great Expanse,
I will go willingly, humble, and
Give myself to the Great Mother
Who resides in the desert,
Just off route 66,
In a place called…
Mercury Flats [my Brigadoon]!

Tribute to Willy Marks

1919: BORN

Hailed from Twentynine Palms:
Traditional youth, brilliant mind,
Read books at early age.
Dark complexion like Hindus of
Bangladesh, handsome beyond words,
Girls and womenfolk swooned.
Ramrod straight in stature, athletic in
Prowess, envied by tribal boys and
Encouraged by menfolk all.

1936: UNIVERSITY

Full scholarship: studied Latin, Greek,
Linguistics, Philosophy, and Literature.
Europe at war, bored with academia,
Dropped out.

1939: UNITED STATES ARMY

Stationed in Dayton, Ohio, cryptologist.
(Looking forward to time in Europe)
"You don't always get what you want," says he.
Learned to smoke good cigars and drink fine wine
Like a White Man.

1945: CIVILIAN AGAIN

Married Elsa Jimenez.
Twenty-odd years worked as informant, translator
With various linguist-ethnologists, including
John Peabody Harrington of Picuris Pueblo fame
Early on. Spent more time drinking than translation.
During this time had two sons: Carlos & Honore'.
Also befriended American anthropologist
Carobeth Laird and her Chemehuevi husband,
George.

1965: DIVORCE

Elsa files for divorce and takes the kids.
Too much drinking, not enough work, always poor.
Willy tries Alcoholics Anonymous, after seven years
Finally achieves continuous sobriety. For
Twenty years worked as odd jobber.
"I worked so many jobs I can't remember most,"
Says he. Librarian, museum curator, bookstore
Clerk, translator, writer for local newspapers,
Tour guide…

1985: RETIRED

Social security but not much else.
Moved in with son Carlos and family, big house,
Three acres, dogs, cats, chickens, bee keeping, fruit
Trees, vegetable gardens, Alamosa, Colorado,
New home, forever home.
[These later years he bloomed like a wildflower –
Became a respected Elder, whose words were like
Honey-coated wisdom, sought by many.]
His life was not perfect like the lives you read in
Fairy tales and children's books – NO, it was a life
Challenged by alcohol, tobacco and diabetes.
"First three horsemen of the Apocalypse,"
Says he.

1998: MENTORING

He became known as a wise man, others came,
Wanting knowledge of the old ways, advice galore,
On translating, best books to read, best crops to

Sow, politics, sociology, philosophy, the meaning of
Life. And of course, such mundane things:
Bicycle repair, gardening, making kites, how to
Talk proper to one's dog.
I came to him by accident while visiting
Alamosa, Colorado. In a coffee shop, asked him to
Borrow sugar from his table.
One thing led to this and that, and he asked me to
Have coffee the next day bright and early.
That day we sat at the coffee shop for hours talking
About life, the Chemehuevi traditions, poetry, reading,
The world.
We left to have a bite at the local Chinese café and
Talked more.
Then we walked, and walked and walked throughout
Downtown, still talking, me mostly listening in
Rapt wonder.
[This man had stamina, me getting tired & saying so]
Evening approached and he asked me:
"Supper with family?"
Spent the evening feasting on corn-on-the-cob,
Black beans, roasted chicken and greens from the
Garden. The day ended at ten-thirty. My head was in
A whirl. Life was good.

1998-2003: VIRTUAL MENTORSHIP

Willy became my defacto philosophical mentor
Through the years that followed. Phone calls,
Emails, letters.
"Regarding Spirit" was his last letter to me
Dated two months before his death, but never sent.
Son, Carlos, found it among his father's things.
Mailed it two years after Willy's death [Oct. 2005].

He also sent back five letters I had written and
Apologized for not answering. Carlos' personal
Note to me described Willy's anguish of being a
Burden on others and condemned to
Assisted living and then hospice. His last month was
One of being confused, completely out-of-his-
Freaking mind, as Carlos explained.

2012: REMEMBRANCE

My memories of a vibrant mind, well read,
Creative, skeptical, challenging authority, even
His own people, will live in my heart until the day
I too will pass into the
"Great wide-open expanse," he spoke about so
Passionately and continuously.
I give the world this tribute of a great and wise man
Whose heart, soul and mind will not be lost in
The dustbin of history.

Our Lady of the Rock

Incipit Prologus

I discovered Sister Maria Paula Acuna in 1998 while researching things about the Mojave Desert. She has and still claims to this day to see the Virgin Mary at a place she named *Our Lady of the Rock*. On the 13th day of every month hundreds of men, women and children follow the great Sister into the desert to watch for signs and portents from the sky. Only Maria Paula can see and speak with the Virgen. Onlookers and the hardcore faithful search the sky for signs from heaven, gazing into the sun and snapping photographs, with Kodak cameras or cell phones, of the cloud formations. Sister Acuna chants, "Blessed be the Holy Virgin," in Spanish, and sometimes Latin.

SANCTA DESERTO

STANZA ONE –

At Mojave turn east
Ward to California City.
Randsburg-Mojave Road
Old 20-mile Mule Team Road
PASS BY-KEEP GOING-DON'T LOOK BACK
Desert Tortoise State Reserve
Borax Bill Park
Hand lettered sign up ahead
"LEFT."
Thursday, 9th June, 2016
1:00 pm (Maybe?)
Windy. 91 degrees. Dry. REALLY DRY!
(Humidity? – where'd it go?)

REFRAIN –

Looking at the sun and the clouds
    (mirando el sol y las nubes)
Praying to the Holy Virgin
    (orando a la Santisima Virgen)
Blessings like rain fall on you
    (Bendiciones como la Llvia caen sobre ti)

SANCTA SANCTORUM

STANZA TWO –

Cheap looking compound,
Trailers, storage sheds,
Machinery.
Sign: CLOSED
(Riddled with bullet holes)
High energy
(Full hydro-electric)
Whence does it come?
No humans.
Creosote, cactus, lizards, dust.
Sounds of nature only, EXCEPT:
Wind pushing a plastic water bottle
Across the sands, dodging
Congregations of desert life.
Mother Maria Paula Acuna
Where are you hiding?
(Inside where it is safe and cool?)
Did not your visions speak of
My imminent arrival today? (Minus the crowds)
All I wanted was a smile,
A touch, a spoken word.

REFRAIN –

Looking at the sun and the clouds
    (mirando el sol y las nubes)
Praying to the Holy Virgin
    (orando a la Santisima Virgen)
Blessings like rain fall on you
    (Bendiciones como la Lluvia caen sobre ti)

EXSPECTO/DESPERATIO

STANZA THREE –

Hanging on the chain link fence
Like the crucified ONE
(My twisted imagination)
In the distance beyond
The cheapened environment
The shiny, white chapel winks
As a jack rabbit runs across
The Holy threshold to the ROCK.
(Which I will never see)
An old white van parked
(Is someone inside? Maybe not)
The eye strain brings tears
Should have come on the 13th.

REFRAIN –

Looking at the sun and the clouds
    (mirando el sol y las nubes)
Praying to the Holy Virgin
    (orando a la Santisima Virgen)
Blessings like rain fall on you
    (Bendiciones como la Lluvia caen sobre ti)

VIGILANTIA/VISUM

STANZA FOUR –

I turn away and gaze, focused
(an hour? Two? More?)
Far beyond the Congregations of
Creosote, cactus, lizard, dust,
And sharpen my eyes
SOMETHING MOVES IN THE DISTANCE!
Animal? Person? Too far...
Its gait is slow and steady
(Hair on arms, neck bristle)
Single note of flute explodes
Across my brain matter
(Full hydro-electric)
Body now shaking, quivering
(Not making sense!)
The (WHATEVER) stops.
Is it gazing back at me?
I snap a picture with my cell phone
Looking at it, disturbing...
Small human figure enshrouded
In circle of bright white.
(Stupid camera phone or reality?)
Something to think about until
The end of my days.

REFRAIN –

Looking at the sun and the clouds
    (mirando el sol ylas nubes)
Praying to the Holy Virgin
    (orando a la Santisima Virgen)
Blessings like rain fall on you
    (Bendiciones como la Lluvia caen sobre ti)

Confessio Fidei Provisoriam
My 2017 Provisional Confession of Faith
Composed in Poetic Narrative Form

On Being Devoutly Religious

In this sense: I AM RELIGIOUS
Behind all the discernible laws
And connections
There is a FORCE that is subtle,
Intangible, inexplicable.
Veneration for this FORCE is
My religion.
To sense that beyond anything
I can experience there is a mystery,
Something my mind cannot grasp,
Whose beauty and sublimity reach me
Only indirectly, is
My religion.
In this sense: (and in this sense only),
I am a devoutly religious man.

On Belief in God – Spirit – What?

The way I see it,
I am in a huge library
Filled with books
In many languages
I do not understand.
I know SOMEONE must have written the
Books, but I do not know who or why.
I dimly suspect a mysterious order in
The arrangement of the books
But I do not know what it is.
Is the source of my library God?
The only thing I know is that
I know nothing. At age sixty-three
I understand the difference
Between TO KNOW and TO BELIEVE.
Am I an atheist?
Atheists know that God does not exist.
I do not.
Those who are conventionally religious
Know God exists. I do not.
But do I believe there is a God?
I am still working on that one –
And hoping God will not hold that against me.
Arthur Schopenhauer was a Pantheist.
He equated God with the forces and laws
Of the universe – seen & unseen.
Baruch Spinoza reasoned that God and
The material world were

Indistinguishable.
He saw our human mind as parts of
God's Mind.
He reasoned, the better you understand
How the universe works
The closer you come to God. He said:
"It is the nature of the mind to
Perceive things from a
Certain timeless point of view."
I think I would feel comfortable
Discussing God with this gentleman
If he was still around.

Free Will and Destiny

Arthur Schopenhauer also said:
"A man can do as he wills
But not will as he wills."
My view is similar.
I am ninety percent determinist.
Our biological makeup, our parents,
Our siblings, our schools,
Our economic status,
The hypothetical forces in our lives that
Unpredictably determine events –
Favorably and unfavorably –
Have an enormous amount to do
With our free will.
Our free will is only free with
All these considerations
Added to the equation.

A Hereafter?

I think like a Buddhist –
But just an inch short of
Buddhahood.
I feel like Yogi Berra:
"If the world were perfect,
It would not be perfect."
When people talk about the Hereafter,
My logic tells me the same thing
About heaven…if there is one.
And I have always appreciated
Mark Twain's inordinate reasoning:
"Most people never learn to
Play the harp of fly."

More Thoughts on God

The only thing I know is that
I know nothing.
Noah Webster defines the word know as:
"To be convinced or certain of the
Truth of something."
HOWEVER – one exception.
Like Sinclair Lewis,
I want to believe there is a God,
And that HE, SHE, IT, is a good guy
With nothing but good things in store
For me when I have served my time
On this planet.
How I see it objectively is this:
We humans are all in the same lifeboat.
That lifeboat is in the middle of an
Ocean with no land in sight.
Regardless how smart we are, how
Wise we pretend to be –
Or how much any of us pretend to know –
None of us actually understand
Why we are in this lifeboat,
Where we came from, or
Where we are going when we leave.
As much as we know, by
Noah Webster's definition, we each live
For a brief moment between

Two Infinities. When I look out from
Our lifeboat, I can assume there is land
Somewhere beyond the horizon.
I can hope. I can believe.
But I cannot know. Relative to
Questions like where we came from,
Why we are here, and where we are going,
What I know, what any one of us
Knows,
Amounts to absolute zero.
If there is a God,
Do I think it matters to HIM, HER, IT
What I believe?
I doubt if anything I might think
Could possibly threaten or insult a God.
Am I going to hell because
I do not buy the bigotry, hatred,
Intolerance, and irrational thinking
That is preached in so many
Houses of worship?
Again, I sincerely doubt it.
I am reasonably certain that any
God I might imagine would be

Quite unlikely to reject me for using
The brain I have been given to
Think and reason independently,
Even if it turns out I am wrong.
Matter of fact, I think it is more likely
That the ones who should be most
Concerned about their fate
Are the church-going bigots
Who pretend to speak for their God
And in the process harm others.
I imagine that would make any God
Extremely angry. Jesus suggested
The world would be a much better place
If we all lived by the Golden Rule.
Remember the exception I mentioned?
Here is something I KNOW:
If each of us treated one another
The way we would like to be treated –
Twenty-four-seven – this world would be
One hell of a lot better place to live.

On Belief

Although I have stated all that I think
Regarding God, I have yet to mention
What I believe – not know…
(Just what I have chosen to believe),
Because I think it makes more sense
Then anything I can imagine,
When I note the fact that we exist at all,
And when I attempt to come up with
Any other rational explanation for existence.
What I believe is that
God is inside of me, inside each of us.
(The Kingdom of God is Within You),
As Tolstoy tried to explain.
And I believe because of that fact

We have the power to choose how we
Look at each day we live
And how we look at what happens to us
During that day. I believe the God (inside)
Has given us the power to react
Positively or negatively to the
Thoughts we are having, to what we are thinking.
Like the old saying:
It is not what happens to us,
It is how we react.
A Chemehuevi Elder once told me:
"Look in the mirror when you are troubled,
That is where you will find the solution."
Whether we will be happy
(Or at least content) during the day,
Regardless of our circumstances,
Or whether we will be sad and frustrated
By our circumstances
Is our choice. I believe we each have
The independent power to choose.
Consequently, the only thing that makes
Any sense to me is to choose
To be happy. So that is my choice.
Do I have moments when
I have to fight off the negative?
Of course, but I know I have
The basic power to do so,
So I use it!
I may be a disguised Buddhist
(Or a radical agnostic):
I believe suffering is inherent in life;
(Mono no aware!)
I know it has been in mine. And
I believe that suffering can mostly be

Found somewhere in the life of everyone.
But I would not express my solution exactly
The way Gautama Buddha did:
"Mental and moral self-purification" –
Because I do not understand what the hell
Self-purification actually means in practice.
But I do believe
We have a mental obligation to the
Incredible GIFT we have been given
To be alive, and to be able to
Think and reason. To be alive,
To be able to reason, to be human
On this tiny Blue Dot of a miracle in a
Universe totally beyond our understanding
Is simply incredible. As Einstein said:
"Acknowledge everyday as a miracle
Because that is what it is."
So each and every day when I see clouds,
The blue sky, the desert and
Mountains around me, the sun, moon,
Rain, even the fact that I woke up again
To see these miracles, I say to myself:
"What a HELL OF A PLACE THIS IS!!!"

ADDENDUM

If you enjoyed this book of narrative poetry, I would be grateful if you would post a review on Amazon, Goodreads or your private blog. The review can be good, bad or indifferent. All reviews are welcome. We independent authors lack the resources of the big publishing houses to raise the visibility of our books. Instead, we rely on our readers to promote our books by word of mouth and writing reviews. See the links to my other works on the next page.

LINKS

Go to my Amazon Author Page for other works I have written and to connect with my BLOG:

https://www.amazon.com/author/benjamindougl ass

You can also connect with me at:

www.mercuryflatspublishing.biz